Shadow

Alex Wong was born in 1988 in London, where for the most part he was schooled, though he spent much of his childhood in Oʻahu, Hawaiʻi. He studied and now teaches English literature at the University of Cambridge. *Poems Without Irony*, his first collection of poetry, was published by Carcanet in 2016, and his original and translated verse has appeared in *PN Review*, *New Poetries VI*, *The Forward Book of Poetry 2018*, and elsewhere. He also edits and introduces the *Selected Verse of Algernon Charles Swinburne* and the *Selected Essays of Walter Pater* for Carcanet Classics. He is the author of a critical book, *The Poetry of Kissing in Early Modern Europe* (2017), and his studies of English literature have appeared in various periodicals. *Shadow and Refrain* is his second collection of poems.

ALEX WONG

Shadow and Refrain

POEMS AND TRANSLATIONS

CARCANET

First published in Great Britain in 2021 by
Carcanet
Alliance House, 30 Cross Street
Manchester, M2 7AQ
www.carcanet.co.uk

A CIP catalogue record for this book is
available from the British Library.

ISBN 978 1 80017 098 8

Book design by Andrew Latimer
Printed in Great Britain by SRP Ltd, Exeter, Devon

The publisher acknowledges financial
assistance from Arts Council England.

With shamfast looke to shadoo and refrayne

These
poems are
designed to be
read using the mouth

Contents

The power of the visible
is the invisible . . .

> Marianne Moore,
> 'He "Digesteth Harde Yron"'

He made me feel again that things are not what they are supposed to be, that the important things are the undefined things—as if one did not know the name of one's love, and so could never find him except by chance.

> Marion Milner,
> *A Life of One's Own*

It is good to love the unknown.

> Elia,
> 'Valentine's Day'

And there are few of us, surely, who do not possess, somewhere in their life, friends of the highest value whom they have barely known—met with once or twice perhaps, talked with, and for some reason not met again; but never lost sight of by heart and fancy. . . . Indeed, this is the meaning of that curious little poem of Whitman's—'Out of the rolling ocean, the crowd, came a drop gently to me'—with its Emersonian readiness to part, 'now we have met, we are safe;' a very wise view of things, if our poor human weakness really wanted safety, and did not merely want 'more'—indeed, like that human little boy, want 'too much.'

Vernon Lee,
'Other Friendships'

I began this letter in a different spirit from that in which I end it; I feel very black and angry within me, at you, at myself, at the absurd mockery of this impotent friendship of ours; 'now we have met we are safe'—! indeed! absurd rubbish! What good has our meeting been, except a little foolish happiness and conceit of sympathy. . .

Vernon Lee,
Letter to Mary Robinson,
Feb. 19, 1881

PART
ONE

As Though to an Old Friend (I)

Given to confidence
          by some chance recollection—
As though you were not the stranger
          you would have come to be,—
I return at times to the feeling I could reach you,
Turning, by a quick remark
          or legible expression,—
Without the calculating hesitancy
          Owed to you now. To think of the remote
Discarnate citadel of Machu Picchu

Prosaically replete
          with human life, supplied
With water, sprung from somewhere,
          plenty of food, and what
The merchants brought to market by now-lost bridges,
Steps over terraces hunching
          up to the rampart's side,
By routes that only scholarship now can plot
          (Tracing remains that do not quite belong,
Which call for explanations—dim conjectures),—

Is easier than to think
          of our association—
Outlying now, but once
          (come, tell me if I'm wrong)
Filled with the surplus of paired energies,—
As other than the far
          secluded fortification,

The inaccessible thing it seems, among
        The insignificant hills, when habit wakes
To an active memory's hacking at dark trees.

Where are the roads that then
                joined to our territory
The rest of the world? Beneath,
                far down, a river's snake
Changes its skin continually—bent near,
But passing, never touching,
                and in no evident hurry.
Are they choked only by time, or barred by mistake,
        Those old ways in from, out to, other life,
That might lead even by devious ways to here?

Though crumbling now, the walls
                are ever more fast secured.
Lethargic tangles mask
                the entries. I have no knife
Serviceable. I am like you, displaced;
And I scan the panoramas
                captured from onboard
Drones that my sceptical memory must contrive.
        And there it is: imperviously immured,
Unnecessarily, in a romantic waste.

With Increasing Agitation

> *... wild cats fighting, at dawn a donkey sobbing ...*

I'm company
      sorry enough,
Like a melancholy seaside donkey
Entertaining hopes
      of humble radishes
And worrying about the greatness of its enemies.

But you come, introducing to the scene
Something of your climate and sheer light,
Vistas of shade; your 'unmistakably real
Feeling for asses',
      or: I am mistaken.

Agreeable reproaches brush me down.
You can easily charge up the old ego like that.
And I'm not free, but glad to learn more pressure,
Deeply hosted. I consent to be

Involved, all this
      diverting shyness shared
In prepossessing tact; and I stand up
Quicker in fresh attention.

        *

After the least struggle,
      I spend myself
In a haemorrhage of new,
      ungainly kindness;
Discover the grammar of getting going,—

Find, not choose,
        the lexicon
From inside the embrace
        of the moments' effort:
A present drive at concert, to secure
Spontaneous equation.

Stuff me with your strangeness: stupid me
In the face of tricky luck.
                      Still, I'm
Six out of seven dwarves, and not
Happy. And we're all six
Feckless and Improvident and Hungry.

              *

Tonight, the quiet disposal of today
In stammering sleep. Down in the personal theatre
We finish the scene, two speakers, and a Ghost.

Pick one part first: the best. Then take the other.
Could we cut either role—and which?
What should be said, by whom, and how do we answer?

The Ghost—a sad case, but convivial—
Prefers, I suspect, a more dangerous solution;
But isn't a speaking part, and wiggles

Out of the reach of inky hands. We go
Without the text. Sharp manners, ready wit
Suffice, till judgement bores through the candle-light.

             *

So I forget myself and talk and talk.
The boisterous speculations come out hard,
Impatient for expression.

The words have never stopped
        resisting, but the sense
Is little impaired for that. It was artless prattle:
Artless, prattle. In the grateful night
Where conversation clambered, you,
I think, misunderstood me right.

Am I to recognise
Some intimated tilting in this strange
Knowing   with respect to the possible?

Finding the appeal of purpose
Obvious   in the unsevere reserve,
I bit the problem hard; our favourite words
Using us, with dubious expertise,
As though they owned the whole, enormous subtext;

And they do.

                    *

A brilliant column slants
Down, so you catch colour
Wearing ideas that are new
                    to one of us.

Prior designs, repeated incomplete;
Needs found early
        for what has not been found—
Inaugural institutes, long got by heart,
They get between. Another doubtful start?

        Can't I
        switch off
        the lamp

                        Of my own
                        pale   magic lantern?

As Though to an Old Friend (II)

Rattling old cassettes
Go into the wheezing old machine.
        Blackish red   as
Semi-diaphanous skin of centipedes
In shovelled soil,   the tape—

        Chewed up and
        Spooled back
Into its tidy coils before,
(It would have been years ago)—retains
Its track; everything works;   but in the rewinding, now,
The motor speeding,
                the degraded end
Snaps at the take-up—
                not to be supplied
Again: and the driven wheels   go round for nothing

Years too late, I took your hint:
At last knew what you had meant. Missing the point
Of your (still putative) ambivalence,
I had missed any ways the exposure of it commended.

Now I suspect you of having been pleased with yourself;
And the parts
        spin without traction.

Consolation (No. 7)

Whenever she makes pragmatical conditions,
Piercing the atmosphere of tendency,
His idle brutes   just up and flee:

Like children with nice principles, when another,
A wild one, draws   the phallic part
And wants to explain what it is,
And give exciting report on that whole activity:

In the uncertain affright
They blow little bubbles in gum
And wait in a circle by the pond, consulting.

Haven't I been the one, and the rest of them also,
Creeping away, afraid of being named?

                    *

She's visiting his country. Her tired steps
Cut across the fields,
Full of cow-life and little bird-lives before,
And quantities of rats among the corn,
Where nothing today will show its head at all;

And now it could be a spare moon's moon.

Still, she can recognise familiar may
Daubing along the limits;
Plots a plan of the road by its various signs
Where trees allow tracing;
And the river that runs too easily its settled course,
And shines in measured curves.

Skilfully vines, pink-bellied and green, go cloak
The iron and plate-glass house, this nature's work.
The inhabitants of all acres around
Are standing there together within,
Or lie together in their several kinds,
Comparing notes.   They are waiting to concede:

But in the spin of a supposed triumph,
Or in the opacity
Of a hot night, or a mist
Of tender misdirections; in taboo
To cover that concession, or confess
And turn it to a jest.

Would it provoke them out of that dead rule
To imagine, feel, how they might please again
The benevolent persecutor   free:
The one that never lost for good the way—

Could she throw in a line,
And they begin to grope
And seem to know the sleeping knack they crave?

*

Kept up the panic for a little while;
Too much commitment, moody hair
Playing up constantly.

                    To be obtuse
Is gratifying at best, not satisfying;
To pass discomfort on, sustain
Both it and a decent bearing, is a strain.

Experience, finished well,
Resurfaced in a twilight of revision:

            Give it a cooler handle
                of even prose.

        It's hardly anything: like
            making the bed.

But somewhere in the house, that fine crying
Sounds even now. It isn't anything like
Making the bed;
                    the bed unmade again.—

Consolation (No. 8)

Against the talk   I used   brute sober taste,
And set like a falling curtain;

Spiralled up the stone of massive stairs:
Up through a layer of dramatic smoke:
Into a level spot above the soiled
District of that intimate trade—

Moon stratum,
                    without politics;
Only limpid law, and nothing turbulent.

    *

Reduced to cleanly order, I
                    can rest, well cooped about,
Measuring shadows, making you hate,

While deafening provisos fly
At all the stiffened webs,
And complicated stars show in a verge
Sloping into the tidy crowns of trees—
Proudly genteel before that dangerous light.

Only, in the waking spells
          out of this fanciful comfort,
I feel the familiar reel   spooling around.
The playing   filters liquid   through these rooms,
Beating patterns deep into my cheap
Singularities.

    *

Back down below, gently those fingers touch
The padlocks, where the fields
Ripple still   under a softening wind.

My broken enclosures there receive
The more solicitation: undeserved,
Not unexpected.

                    As in a haunted house,
You trust your moving weight to my slippery timbers,
Carrying cordial heat to the lame outlines
And relics of this strange abandonment.

                    *

Is it too easy—to catch up all the guilt,
To make this fault a blame, and never explain
Its reach, and all the history it engages?
To let the worldly cause
Go by, forgotten, accounted random or slight?
Some 'tenuous' thing
            was a 'matter of life and death';
Meaning, it is
            both one thing and the other.

Is it too simple now,
                    will it prove the worse at length,
To take the chance of a tacit restoration?—
Allow it to be made out it was all
A freak of mere interior glitch alone,
Its own effect, as though
                    of faulty electronics:
Reasonless, periodical malfunction?

                    *

Not confident, but with
                defiant affliction ebbing,
Can I bundle up and leave, allow
By increments my steps
                to free, loosen again?

Orange leaves lie rustling   crisp across
Every new tread I let my ravel down,
Reluctant, as the crackling hesitancies
Pester the senses eager for a sign.

Invited, the long stair
                falls to the glowing traffic.

About Consolations

'Come, come, my wench,' said her father, soothingly, putting his arm round her, 'never mind; you was i' the right to cut it off if it plagued you; give over crying; father'll take your part.'

Each blunder, every unseen failure, sticks,
And it carries on its life, a separate point.
But shame, accruing, proves   transferable—
Elides with other consciousness of poor
Deportment, other   doubtful seeds in chaos.

Atonement for one blemish on the mind
May fade some others. But in this crooked scheme,
Inner events   are disproportionate
And will not keep their scale.   Are we ever right
In speculating what will count against us?

Someone's bag   brushed lightly against my back.
For a moment I thought, without turning, it was you.
No one should ever be   relied upon
To speak in tones or flash the looks that launch
The wave of general, instantaneous help.

As Though to an Old Friend (III)

Could you, the not understood, could even you—
Not the remains upset again for me
        (Restored, it seems, to an old accustomed role—
        With the now-remembered threat of incipiency
At every word),
            but the unencountered you
Return to me, and I
            to you in alarming prose,—

Could I send you out of the teeming
            traffic, and would you go?—
To the rambling house in the wayless hinterland,
Where there is no conduct; there is no enterprise:
Only their images?
            There you will find myself

'Perched up on chairs at a distance, in a large parlour,
Sitting moping   like three or four melancholy birds
In a spacious volery'.
            Little is said down there.
But back in prose the adjustments would be made.

And you, having come so far,
            you would be like

The archaeologist who, having dug
An empty tomb, or an ancient temple, finds

Later, in quiet sobriety, in a far
Museum, the missing bodies; the missed, imagined
Statuary, staring;—
                         and I would be like

The dumbly appealing forms in the novel place,
Telling you nothing new unless you asked,
Giving you what, though never on display,
You had always nearly known;
                         and you would be like

Are you serious? And back in town I would take,
With proper ritual, your implications.

Night Thoughts (I)

My nation without house
                    goes stumbling on,
Passes again
       between
The visible curtains,
Into the faster shade.

It moves in the fulfilment
Of feelings not in motion,
       dreams in amber.
There is a feeling that is coming home.

The very stance of that love
Should discommend description.
It is a large perfection
Of an unknown work
              that lessens in your sight.

Night Thoughts (II)

My model ark washes
               from its latest dream
Towards another reading of you.
A single high-crowned wave could suck it
Mouth-like into hope.

               But none of us
May really choose our fools;
Nightingale, elephant, rat, familiar pig,
Our fellow-travellers
               nesting in the hold,
Ready to hope for the best and reproduce.

Plain Speaking

*In the last muffled moments of a telephone conversation, or at the
end of dinner in a restaurant as the candle burns fitfully, some
words are said to have been said, or, if they were not actually said,
they were not denied, which, in the circumstances, they should have
been if they were not to be honoured. 'But I took it as a promise, you
know I did, don't say you don't because you do, you do.' And then
comes the great untruth, 'I shall never believe you, ever again.' For
how, if the victim stopped believing, would the disappointment so
dearly loved be possible again?*

Richard Wollheim, Germs

I.

Where are you calling from, six feet away,
Sitting and talking there? Candour is no
Blank, immaculate, anodyne, but plays
A game of invitations and evasions;
Held in common, the unsaid means the most,
When every step implies a prized admission.
Sincerity cannot be the inert
Expansiveness of an easy unconcern,
But a shore of narrow inlets;
      tentative waters finding
Entries unguarded, opening under rocks.

Darkened
      in the rough rooms
To another, starker brightness,
Gingerly the water
      starts to make them out:
Sounding with itself

the under-places, proves
The ridgy contours overhead
With resonance and light. But the tide goes out;

The cavities now left to their empty shame,
The heavy seaweed fills the static air
With its odour, waits for buoyancy again;
The vaults lean uncaressed by the faulty light
That lapped, evolving, like smoke on the walls:
Gleams in the dark are prone discarded bottles,
Floated in, now dead on sand.

How long till we are safe? Are we going there?
I think there is no safety in the thing
But what we make by instants, caught between
This strange familiarity,
            and this old, familiar strangeness,
Back like a dithering tide. But where do you call from?

II.

A push of instinct: inarticulate, thus
The more precise in gain,
            and delicate in motion,
Making way by undertaken stress
Of looks and tones. You have a tact
For coy intrusions, squibs of impudence.
Equal, a consultive reticence
Flits at the margins of the affinity.

And over its sifted records Disappointment
Hunches, always ready for the word,
Still restively surveying its accounts.

'A genius for sympathy': at what cost?
Do you understand the unmeasured benefit
Of the new but dubious shapes
     in the stretch between;—
Like draperies barely seen
     of the wind when it catches
Weights of a monotone of tender rain,
Bright, imperfect folds
     in a dim space:
A heavy brightening, almost missed,
Moving along the expanse,
As though un-present hands went passing over;—

—That what we lose in the regular clarity
Of commonplace operation,
We gain, or can redeem,
In the hazardous clarity of this plain speaking,
Always and always less and less plain?

Portions and Parcels

I.

Translated loosely from those nights
       and the first long earliest days
To a present
     surely
     fairly gained,   a short
Decade spent, and suddenly complete,

I find myself attending, leisurely,
Myself back there with you
      (was it almost you?)—

Talk   full as an egg . . . . and falling
Always on our feet, we were
A little sentimental in our speech;
Less so when doing things, or pretty near.
Missing dinner, even.
                Better not grow

Into the old   costume again,—
Sitting, saying things,
Mildly,
     as though with little emphasis;
Always to one purpose.

II.

Not long before Experience cometh teasing,
Smart, if not serene, with its old conceit,
To feel itself irrelevant this time—

A dozy traveller, finding things
Are not exactly as the book implied:

Looks around for the nearest bridges,
Motorway services;
              can make
A comprehensive study of the text
Again,
              polite descriptions out of date;
But cannot get direction;

Drives the minibus lonely, stepping down
At intervals to try out the new camera.
Maps fold over, beat themselves in the wind,
Tear at the fingered margin. Gadgets fail.

Inexplicable Ocean stands
Wrong,
              in the place of town:
Everything spreading into frightening blue.

III.

A listening, waiting mouth
Addressing me over space:
Smoothly now it sucks the missing time
Into the fragile zone:

A little space of hours
Opened out on a wish
And its never promised law.

The awkward frame is dressed
With measured bits of real,
Appealing things—some lovely accidents
Touched on the quicker passage;

A volatile atmosphere: it
Lightens without noise—
                    great, fuck-off clouds
Cruising around, condensed
Of novel metaphysics—
                    which we urge
Inside, to encounter, reassured,

Abroad:
        when Doubt,   (on the *qui vive*, as ever),
Doing its regular beat, creeps into range
With policy and cautionary tales.
Easier, safer, chain the affectionate beast?

IV.

A band of bored nuns, out and about,
Far out afield, abroad in the night fens,
Cover the ways, disturbing guilty hope.

One dark sister,
          going her dismal round,
Puts a pathetic noise
          into the jazz-bag:

Another puzzle. New, disobliging clue.
A doorstep situation; your
Not listening in the café: anything.

Buzzing between dead spells, at home in jars,
With a diluted glow in the halogen light,
Little soiled tickets of imagined good
Like stupid butterflies   are set aside
In separate custody
          and will not harmonize.

v.

You mentioned, I remember, trivial things;
Obvious, natural things. Of course I turned
About in a frozen panic
          of hotted linen, sprawled
Limp and wrinkled in the mental tub,

Having it all again, as though
In slightly bigger type; would manage, twist—
To make a point
          to miss;   keeper of messy,
Punitive fairy stories.
                              Sitting up late,

It seemed   as though vague sounds replied
To my fit of purple listening. Dried-out voice,
Silent,
          inhales to find   a wandering music.
Fragile sounds
Seep through the padding,
Enter the room. I make myself very sorry.

VI.

Soft light
          through the curtains
                    can divert
Emergent consciousness from the low
          glug-glug, as

Morning sinks
Everything
Evening
Dug for,
          and will again—
A harrying idea, the failed joke—
I heading one more time
          for my pumpkin state.
Just getting another short night done.

Day-break, did it appear, might really end
That campaign long frustrated? But I'd spend
My last way out, safe bet,
In shilly-shally years,
And always miss my happy disadvantage.

VII.

Like a domestic cat
Hopping into a series of open boxes,
Your remembered conversation then
Dropped right in
          with its animated weight,

Moving among bare spaces,
          coming always
Up to my sheer anxieties:
          nudging nose
Getting home   into the tender spots,
Working its mobile news deeper inside,
Leaving its reasons all about my sleep.

And then it beds down to dream in the dustbin there,
Brightly reposed, the tiger side
Easier, quieter.
               Bit my finger, the little
Love, and left a mark.

VIII.

Down here in the Blitz at night, when the trains retired,
The electric current switched off   on the lines,

Over the platform edge
          Londoners spread—to pad
Spaces along the rails;
          stretching between the two
Hammocks for children: inches off the floor.

A fresh nocturnal scene in the metropolis:
Passing in orange light
          down a sooty throat
Our train excites itself to a sleepy scream.

I had been easing to an end
     For three
          good days
     The two
          bad weeks
I had spent alone; long fits of gloomy sofa.
And now the spell was starting to seem set.
We came back tired again. You unpacked again.
You stayed another sleep. I lay between

The peaceful lines, accompanied secure,
But conscious of a charge
          known even in suspension—

Danger of what we have seen so many times
Come hurtling out the tunnels:
Out of the dark: shriek over where we lie,

Secure—no trains, no current—
                                    loosening into the night.

IX.

Black Bear comes forward massively over a hill,
One shaggy, fiery ulcer
Of big wrath.

It tears the padded night in a worrying manner,
Claws numbing and white, and looks so wild;
Unable, in fact,
            to act at random;
Flexible god, with claims in all the new places.

I miss
            places
I never
            completely imagine.—

There's an indoor bridge out there I'm not to cross.

Attention broke on you,
    Turned over asleep—I woke
Myself a shade in almost saying so:
    You here, going missed
Amid the uneasy comfort you respire.

Here in the room,
Whole and still
You lie like a strange nut:

A strange one, of dimensions
Past all possibility

Of estimation; hard
     and present to my lack:

Or a garden of warm and weighted force
Out of which emerge
     some little noises,—
But not the Black Bear that comes back, savage and bouncing,
Looking to arrange dinner.

X.

Through those earliest nights, back to the first,
When nervous weather wraps them; guessing charms

Kiss the near corners of the room; the stillness
Has not burst or shivered, but the long
Practice of the sure
      routine is disallowed—
My ancient solitary reign;—

The former story, its blithe
      projection resting curled
Alongside: hardly there; but over there;

While they collapse
      into the spacious risk,
And trail into another domicile
Unguessed before, the one unproven purpose;
Tuck up the future in this infancy

Of contact to confirm.

Winter 2018–19

On the Waterfront

The whistling stones have a second moon
That ripples. Wooden things creak on the water.
A red light, shining high up, shivers below.

Things the charlatan eye, as though they were
Intelligent auxiliaries, can put
To order and use. We, with great application,

Are speaking through the night air and the spray;
All forms a window, thickly present, that draws me
Slippery into the possible, as entails

You. Sensations of the assailant scene
Make me an optimistic mystagogue,
And the more particular this night in which

We dedicate, across these auguries,
Heroic attentiveness, the more it seems
We may have the right to think that in time to come,

When I, in fact, may be a lone resorter
Back to this specificity—that then,
The ordinary rules might not apply.

Adjustment (I)

The thought had never occurred, she might have died
In a place the mind, to the limit of its power,
Could see by knowledge; not a hospital bed,
Easy to generalise in a basic fancy,
But that bed, in that room, where in a game,
Played with her daughter, whom I no longer know,

I used to search in cupboards, and later hid,
Doubting at first if we should pass the door
Of this new domain, but coaxed; and where I still
Recall being led, one morning, coyly in,
To ask her husband, of whom I was afraid,
What he would like for breakfast, lying in that bed.

Hawaiian Fragment

    attempt at an English version

A light, light wind of subtle misted rain
Sighs of a love,
        love with a mourning in it.
The Malana'i wind
Moans of its love to men,
And it murmurs to women of love.

The wind goes rustling in the leaves,
Saying that where it goes
        are the coolness and the damp.
Chilled by the damp
        are the parts within—
By the hindered stream of that voice; remembrance,
Cold, as if left to soak in chilly water.

It is the welcome voice sticks in the mind,
Remembered as gratuitously there;
Recalled to the mind, a flower for ornament:
The friend now gone, gathered up.

As Though to a Childhood Friend (I)

'girlgrace'

Your bedroom, bed, hard floor, the ceiling fan,
Mosquito screen.—
      Also, you liked to obtain
Often, or do without,
      the special permission
That let us lounge
      watching the television
With a packet of crackers   in your parents',
Later your mother's, enormous bed
With its less familiar clothes resisting
Under the skin
      in the sticky heat.

And mine, my own room at home, old room;
Redundant bunk-bed's metal poles,
Painted, glossy blue,
      and cheeping under the grip;
Hot air balloons on the covers; —where broke out
That one most rancorous fight, one night,
In the lower bunk,
      a discord over rights
To a teddy large as we were then,
Nearly;
      it was owner *vs* guest:
Apparently.

Tearful dispute; you reached
      a limit, and   you wailed.
In the dead of night your mother had to be called;
Summoned, all up

                    the twisting bluffside ways
To get you, take you home in a blaze
Of righteous rage.
              Morning: the telephone;

Taken, at last—as
              far as the curling cord
Would lengthen out of earshot, in a corner.
Watching the ants on the peeling paint, very sorry.

                    *

So often there lurked a third; cynic or blank,
Less blank than a bear, more cynical.
              I think
Of an afternoon with cookies and warm milk
Under your desk
              with your friend who never liked me;
Jealous playmate, who complained;
Complained and was returned a non-committal,
Nonetheless touching endorsement, overheard
From the bathroom
              or in my roaming outside the windows.

And that other:
              on the floor one night—we two
In your small bed together—watcher who put
Too worldly a gloss on our tentative closenesses.

Was our contact subtler then, above her head,
Or the more a performance?
I think both.
I never met her again, but how often, still,

I wonder, has she been
        the sharp unseen watcher?

                *

There are seasons when my dreams return
To recreate you, seeing you not as you were then,
Tomboy of ten—
        voluminous t-shirts
Borrowed from your father, vasty glasses,
Bottle-base wide and thick—
        wide-eyed,
And the grace of not much caring,
        going with
Feeling;—there was an ease, an easy
Wideness I've
        been outside ever since;

Though it's there in a vestige, then, when I see you
Not as I knew you ever once before,
Not as you must, but as you might be now—
And wouldn't, wouldn't be;
                        to whom: all this.

The night before your wedding: we walk in the dark.
You feel uncertain. I give no advice.
By the side of a lake, with something understood,
You disappear. They all ask, but I tell them nothing.

On Escalators (I)

Had you, as just as well you
                    might have, taken the stairs, and
Not the escalator (out of service),
You would have missed this strange banal surprise,

The dead sensation in the join
Of the standing step and the foot, the small
Jar of adjusting balance, stalling speed,
Buoyancy lost, when, gliding
                    over the edge of the plate, you
Mount the first, shallow, irregular
                    steps, surprised by your own flat-
Footedness.—

        After a time,   an old significant Presence
Comes to be, happens to be,
                        present again.
Neither mistakes the measure, both
Peruse the auspices,
                and nonetheless
Among the new mundane
Accommodations furnished each for each

(The moral jettons both dispense
In meeting, none of any external worth),

Some lifting force   they don't expect   is missed;

—Which neither will discuss.   Once I had thought
(Later I have imagined) that with you
Backward adversion
                    could ever assemble anew
What had been left, not lost,
                    and that the same
Dispelling candour, flattering liberty,
Would do again what old experience
Makes one feel it ought:
                    don't give me that;
I've known you a long time: the kind of line
It seemed would always be available.

On Escalators (II)

The cuboids fall, clean on the beat, away
(Betraying at their fall the slight
Curvature on their baring upright sides)
Into a middle span, where the travelling chain
Look stationary:

                   till every step succumbs
At the levelling-out; distinguishes; and files
Neatly down to an even plane, now fed
To a landing plate—its limit of steel teeth.

A suave lustre is falling soft
And weightless, banded, on the scuffed
Ridges of each travelling tread.
Just there, and it seemed then more than ever,
It would have given a certain pleasure
To run a furled umbrella's spindle
Across them, lightly, as you would run
A comb along your lips with an absent mind.

As Though to an Old Friend (IV)

A strange incumbent, this slight figure of you
Pacing about my ways. Most others flit
Unlively down less-travelled corridors

To places of their own, while it stalks through
All, even the new rooms. Will you know nothing of it,
If ever we pass on firmer, secular floors?

As Though to Robert Louis Stevenson

'And when we are alone, we are only nearer
To the absent'.
                    RLS,
I doubt whether you should be envied:
                    more or less
Contemptuously, at best; my usual reverence
Notwithstanding. Must I believe you meant it?

And yet, on the other hand . . . is there a
Distinction to be made,
                    as you might have granted,
Between the simply absent
                    and the signally absented?
To which side the mind falls alone could make all the difference.

Emendation

Then you created your beloved
Out of roots and wrecks.
It was nothing: a wish that flowered, a tulip of air
There on the table; amusing for a time,
Then less so, and then gone, leaving behind
This residue of the anterior me.

That was your share
Of natural, supernatural if you like,
Power, that period: I even liked being there—
Threatened by the strong gaze of that sun,
The granite thumbs of that divinity:
But you're less capable than God, and I'm not
Your creature now, it squeezes down to a principle.

Nevertheless, my mind, like a listless eye,
Falls often over records not without charm.
Or say, the memories dance with the motion of gas
Around me, odourless and invisible.
Uncertainties, which taunt, can also tempt.

The desert place traversed by better light
(Which never fills it), all the old dubious blends
Are being searched again for the genuine thing,
For the good there was—that seems, when it half appears,
At times almost to give out largely again
Onto the stiffened views now loosening:
Vivid against the glass. There is even a breeze.

New lies rankle in their new injuries,
The old ones palely vex. Sentiment will.

As Though to an Old Friend (V)

Only in part
          redacted fact,
You old intractable thing, entire—
And all the likely fable-lore
Component in the whole—you stood:
And so you stand,
          less known, or more;—

Stand off: 'here comes
          the Reality Principle, your
Old enemy, with whom you have had such fun':
Like that,
          but you;
          but worse; and with a smile.

Unlikely fiction, let's agree, though hard:
Opposing, manifest.
                    And all bets always
Placed on a winning way of pushing luck
And losing—
          in the end, wearing out patience—
Bye-bye, Love, like a song,
                    and so long, Succour:

Moments of review, round smart again,
The footwork winding to a posing halt,
When you see the comedy
          may have taken you in—

Trust disappears
        and the earnest child
Must set its desperate covers on stumps of life;
Or you fold
        to your high indifference, Empress-mind
Of silk, concerning affairs
Of the raucous crowds that push at the rails in the square,
Abounding in the talk of life.

But when you were in,
                you had,
                you *had* to have
An overriding claim,—so plain
A title,—first,
        primeval dibs on
Minutes' chances—any—dodging into
View, rolled into play;

Persuasively, if not convincingly
        (design it may have been)
Made either as if you gave or didn't give
The idiomatic fuck.

You remain
        my favourite character from Ibsen,
On the basis that one doesn't count the Duck.

A Provocation

Given up to your disdain
As a holiday to rain,
Don't leave me, or lock me, down here with the other statues,
Dwellers in cubicles; but train
Some agitated thoughts,
          a penetrating beam
Of analytic feeling,
On my denuded failings—
As once on the more offending of my virtues.
Shine on, self-gratified
          in the ricochet gleam.

Sick of this arrested pain
I'd rather be exposed again
In those bloody old migrainous jungles of keen distaste,
Heady and busy. Then—I could restrain
Your mindedness of me
          with a curious fancy-knot
Of flattery, quick distress,
False-hearted cleverness,
Devotion, rancour. Better to be disgraced
Than just to lack the grace
          you do allot.

Two Fragments from Tibullus

I.

Whenever love has called, have I been hard
To its tender evocations?
And therefore when the fatal hour comes
Venus, I hope,   will personally conduct me
Down, over dark, to the land called Elysium:

Venue for choric pleasures, so I read.
Roving around that place,
Consorts of little-throated birds will make
Agreeable sounds, I venture.

Cinnamon's said to be common there, though no one
Cares to spend any art in growing it,
And over the whole wide space there nod
Perky roses, never past their best,
Emphatically scented, fed by the generous soil.

Assorted, one young person by another,
Of either sex,
All go about
Their play in pairs—assiduously join
You know the kind of battle;

For there go those who have suffered the visitation
Of covetous Mortality while they
Were loving: doing or desiring. They wear,
To indicate this honour,
         myrtle looped in the hair.

But the residence appointed for all those
Who behave badly
Is deeper, deeper down—
Extending flat beneath a densely
Insulating night.
          The rivers slurp
Blackly around it. And the Fury whose
     Tussled hair
     Is made of snakes
Raves; and all the faithless gang
Bolt, forever dispersing; and that dark shape

In the dismal gate-way is the sentry dog,
The one with the snake-set mouth,
Hissing outside the brassy porch.

If anyone attempted to divert
My own special friend,
Crossing their guilty fingers I might just find myself
Held up for a few nights longer out of town:

I hope that's where
They'd end up.

II.

I was hard in desperation: I said
The way we parted suited me just fine.
Now that kind of bravado seems
Impossibly remote.

I'm flung out, like a top
      spun over a level floor,
Lashed
      over and
      over
By a boy with a wicked technique
      and a quick arm.

Burn away,
      screw down,
      screw up my wild
Spirit of pride, so I'll never talk
Such glorious trash again: come train
My undomesticated words.

Adjustment (II)

Though when it was denied that I could mean it
The protestations flung to puncture cool
Quicker than this (then out of range) contortive
Conscience unsticks,—one usually agreed

When later asked. Easy to re-confess
You never meant it when the pressure falls,
And gravity, between two presences
In careful poise, resumes its normal reign.

The truth (mistaken) is that you would not
Mean it *now*. But you would not say it now.
You meant it at the time. Racked as I sense it

Still, in this calm—recalling the sensation—
How can I make the fact stay where it was?
The words, too? And no more such coming soon.

The Shower Scene

When the bathroom door swung inward—
Having been left ajar,—
Gathering force to knock
Sharply   onto the bath's enamel brink;

And when, at the third stage, as I count it now,
I started again to think,
        regarding it, I could—

(As in a fourth stage I
Discover I did)—divide
Three phases in the process of that shock:

All passing within
The moment when I turned, and the running foam
Had not been actually found
        painful in opened eyes:

First, automatic fear at a surprise
In this most solipsistic intimacy
That shuts out any sense
Of anything not to trust;

And then the unreflecting certainty,
Vivid and reassuring—while its sound
Played out, and in the way of its cool gust,—
Who it must be.

Then last, and more than mostly, I realize,
Taken in by that presence,
        and replaced
By this affronting stare of vacancy,
That all this month I've been alone at home.

As Though to a Childhood Friend (II)

memory fragment

Is 'friend' the right word? You used to tie me up
With skipping ropes and assail me with sharp things.
I think there was something in it.

... But was it you, or was it some young lady
Of sweeter disposition (I think *you*,
Though the face and voice are gone), the afternoon
With the rusty borrowed knife?

In our own enclosure of ocean pool among rocks,
Slippery black,
     and the perching sea-cucumbers
Glutinous gloss-daubs over them, squirtable,—
I hope not hurting them,
     their woundable bodies;

Just one more day there, but for your big knife,
Illicit plaything, which you said your father
Had given you
     but hid behind a towel;
Serviceable for limpets and the like.

And swimming with you there, in the sheltered place
That swelled—had us rocking, your
     long hair on the water,
As waves came pressing inward through the gaps,—

Going under the surface, down where the sand
Roiled a little, gentler than beyond,—
Eyes opened in the salt-water,
           the knife in my hand,
At the opening of a dark hole in the rocks
Thought I came face to face with a moray eel:

Let the knife fall,
           thrashed off in a voiceless panic,
Made for the beach or the open water,
Sore and hoarse with the swallowed salt.

Must have been a sight.

As Though to an Old Friend (VI)

There seemed
So much more weight
In the weightless shadow that dived
With a slight vibration over sills and lintels
Down the sheer side of four bright storeys in white

Than in the buoyant mass of the single bird
That shot from over the crest of that plaster side.

And could it have been like this,
That time, in that other, now impossible city
Which used to be my home—may still be yours?

The dark shape plummets away
At a hard right-angle, spurts
Across the ground when it levels; and the bird
Carries on as before—holding its course for a time
Before it passes out of scope. For a time

It seems the same, as if no event had been.
But I saw the shadow drop: and it may well be
That really it was never the same again.

Misgivings

To give and give nothing,
               give no ground, and give
Almost as if it were no
             offer at all,
You give in
        through the fog
        a little by little;
Through the deep foliage,
            fronds of the coast, inland;

Boughs, a little apart,
Sigh, or it seems, in a settling-back
As a curl
        over quiet eyes
        in still disquiet,
In a dark light of those moments' grace from the haul,—
The shine's growth
        diminishing on the strand
In a rhythm, its wash of gloss.

We tack offshore, a space
Clear of the reef,
        not totally at a loss,
With our spoiling cargo bound for somewhere else;
Letting the time go, stayed
           at this surprising

Instance of the real
In the waste of the too-familiar
Element, here withstood: element
Now at length too much one thing with the washing
Overboard of a coasting ocean-mind.

A fortunate isle; not fortunate, should I say—
Fortuitous.

      Canoes, venturing vessels,
Tender out,
      stay far;
      and the land has shadows
Brandishing ribbons of colour in ocean wind
On a bluff where the smoke curls over
                  dark, and over away.

From a flat horizon, as from old
Unrecollected traumata, the waves
Nag at the pending craft,
Passed on their way to you and yours,
Appeasing, or impatient.

        In their cradle
Gently we rest,
      as if we were ready
For any embarking hands to appear,
Or bartering hands, on the gunwale.

Something moves.

Already, the new flora floating in.
Is it contact or contagion now?
Rootlets groping
            in a moaning throat:
Great

Elephant ears of tenting foliage
Fertile from a new anxiety—blurts
Of rubbery leafage, huge,
                        bruised, in a fruiting,
Suffocating speech.

———————————————

This is not the freight. We tacked offshore;
And the wind, one night of torches, voices, blown,
Played our sails. We have drifted.

X of our number had gone ashore.
One rowboat gone, and the compass no earthly help.—
Put it like this?
            And this is not the freight:
Had I something to say, and a way, I would say it
In prose. And yet I want to make it sound.

Sometimes to state
                the obvious—
Rivet too much enforced—may be the most
Disorderly offence. Can I make it sound?
That truce held in a trance. Every dawn, the land
Lay there at tether, close in its fog,
In a roadless ocean.

               I can break
Figures now, as then the denser illusion.

Derision,
          a component of your play;
Or was the play no more than a mitigation
Of that more real derision,—shall I say?
Flaring of disdain, incredulous;
Theatrical: 'Don't make me get tough with you'—
          and the quickly softening voice . . .
The cool-it-cowboy tone
               wings every word,
Like birds in air that labour
               and swerve in air—
Schools of ships in a changing wind,
Driven askew;
          pretended liberty.

For me there is no
               more immediate you:
Or no more and no more—the immediate you.
The flora budges out rasping.
The taproot fumbles in the stomach's pit.

Indications

Such a costly faith, I know,
         I was in my buds.
Studies of cowslip,
Studies of rose
Grew to a barking life:
         to my scarlet roots
I'll go again, restrictive among graves.

Uncertain Light

Under my own sun, souvenirs fade a little,
Lose their reference,
                    go unmoored,
As if there had never been any grasp at all,
              any stance, any title.—
What is it for which I cannot see the wood?

Later it seemed we had never been there at all;
Some amplitude the less certain side
Of a blindness,
              shady in light of another sun;
Uncaving, hollowed under the lancing light
Of stars, their own;
                        their open spaces
Found in the late light, and those moving
Groves devoted:
              seen the once, then only
Once and *once* again—no more than nearly
Palpable. And now,
The passage lost, and the ghost-tracks in the fog.

Is it given up now, dead wood, whatever token
Gave down into the shadows cast
By that different sun, or thickening under those
Different stars?
              And what grew there: any chance
Of any cutting coming back,
With cossetting, to life—reviving shoots
Enticed a little toward this paler source
Of my more customary days?

Under these stars
     and this familiar sun
(Mine), the warmth of another, others' prick-work,
Came with you, in a blinding, mild
Elision;
     with a playing round about
Of uncouth angels in orbit, yours—
Another total: order spun from one
Centre, announcing vessel.
              Each of both
A coinciding stranger host.

That other sun updrew to itself far off,
As water in air,
     one wishing, alien tree,
Responsive. You can read the history
Of a second sun now gone, and the slow reverture;
Twist in the wood, fixed in,
     where it grew for a second light.

Over and Over

Each time we start afresh may be the last.
Two minds have made
        one cloven Penelope,
Divergent every night—
                two rooms, two beds,
One dark Penelope;
                four hands, two only
Silently returning to the woven
Work alone in the dark, loosening threads.

Still Life with Mirrors

I'll hide your vestige in the suggestive volumes
Of any bo-peep mirror,
Though I know that any stow-away closed in there
Stays only as though a drifting picture, slowly
Adrift, with no more blood than blithe white china.
And if in cleanly ice
There is any retention of ripples,
From the outside this is only to be guessed.

Indefinite marches, without line or lord,
Long as the longer side
                    of a dreamer's life,
The region of limit shall be dressed
With all the typical strewings—sacrifice
Of all embarrassing troubles; dark danegeld.

The borderlands loosen out large, and glare
Capacious,
            when a peering face comes near—
Coupled, covert
            behind itself to spy
Slyly around those corners of its own:
Obstructed by this recollected self,
Once in your living way.

                Once, we broke
Music as bread. My letters outdo each other.
I miss the misspelt messages of met looks.

                    *

Abroad there's divination nonetheless,
By force or art.
      Remembered emissaries,
Those paper aeroplanes into the void,
Relay belated maydays; are enough,
Like any glister of you, to slow my pace
At the instant, drag the feet.

Expressions, yours, too little understood,
Return uncalled, with a stirring of their scent
As from a rich-laid tomb
Newly unsealed, and spring untravelled roads
Of open country. Every one declines
Dead short upon a point.

          *

What effort may be virtuously spent
To still the virtue from a choice distortion?
Or how drain off the latter-day mystique
And not the godhead
          which the overpassing
Rag of dawn would have us satirize?

What if I read false dreams
          to independent life?
This is my purest material, conveyed
With so or so much derision;
          such as I add to,
Knead and part, unable just to hold.

          *

Could I hide you in the dissembling mirror,
Any and all, to be always out of sight,
Kept in the lively vanity—mock shadows
Draping and muffling all the less forward edges
There in that answering shade?
To be always out of sight, behind

The offensive form,
                    surprising, caught
In the foreground—its confronting unity,
As though it came from beyond one; not

Regulated (at a guess) from the inner
Chamber and made to be met, like the optimistic
Estimate pressed to the world,
                    the face
Meant to be, smooth to be seen:
The sugared-almond, extrovert vitrine . . . .

But who shall do the being, out of which
This double-going blows?

                    . . . . Is it only this—
Poetry—wants a last, original world
Or some prized element,
                    left vestigial here,
Fully to mean in perpetuity
Its miracles   keeping lost   behind the sheet?

Should I look for a daylight footprint, moulded sharp?—
Sharper than this sheer presence apart, which I

Too shiftily propitiate, in fits
Of patency
        when I coddle souvenirs,
Try charming ghosts—and cannot safely name—
In a judicious present all my own?

Too soon the eyes get out of date,
Willing to pay themselves to see the hem
Of just one angel as it fades. The pores
Of the psyche's darkening sieve are coarse;
Too coarse, too loose to hold for long
These perishable supplies.

                    * * *

            What always stares
Square from the glass, oblique from glass in glass—
This cover, stark
Impediment (open eyes
Following always),
            fixes me. Apart

Her Other-Nature stands:
                invisible stone
Of motion; threatening, like a jealous god,
The ambition of a glance that will not win.

Ivy Walls

What a pleasure to see
The flung and the lifted
Waves all over
Your green, thick cover
       of ivy—

Expressive,
       as it has always seemed,
The genial swathe;
       albeit the fluent wind
Comes under and through it
From the outside,

Insinuating;
       and in the end,
The hard, stone angles and the planes
Solid beneath it
       need to be better borne

In mind, and your foursquare immobility;
And the blind in every window
       out of the wind's
Reach, on the other sides of well-shut panes.

PART
TWO

Fancypiece (I)

Children would dance in that soft uproar,
Spring from the doors, and spin there.

Resting in worn-down heels
                    after their game of labour,
Strewn on the rugged heights
                    moist with the summer rain,

They will shudder, once or twice, with healthy fear,
Qualified by wryness or by wine,
And gaze at all the trophies of their play
Scattered, unexplained, in the dark mud.

A Spell to Lure Apollo

    after Conradus Celtis (1459–1508)

Vacate your seasonal hideaways,
  Phoebus—deviser
      of the charming zither.
Down the high slopes of Helicon:
  Come for a trip
      to these chilly margins.
Sir, we invoke you, as you see, in verse.
      You like poetry.

Look at our blowzy Muses now
  Gaily preparing:
      how nicely they warble
Under this bitter and icy pole.
  Come to our country,—
      untilled, as untutored
In cultivation of your resonant lyre,
      Debonair deity.

The graceless boor, still innocent
  Of classic glamour,
      the lore o' the Romans,
Soon, beneath you, bright pedagogue,
  Shall learn to write verses,
      fresh as when Orpheus
Sang to his antique audiences—not
      'Sclusively human:

Murderous brutes, and the nippy deer,
　　And even the towery
　　　　trees of the forest
Followed demurely while he picked
　　The wires to a tune
　　　　with wizard fingers.
So come across the desert ocean, glad
　　　　　　Of a new challenge.

Sir, over here. Long since, from Greece
　　You travelled to Latium,
　　　　hauling the Muses,
Meaning broadly to disburse
　　The arts you favour.
　　　　Now we petition:
As you came then to those Italian lands
　　　　　　(Conspicuous precedent),

Make up your mind to rove up here.
　　Come to our grating
　　　　shores. By your office
Make all our barbarism of speech,
　　Mortally cherished,
　　　　up and vanish:
Make all the dark, the whole wide cage of murk,
　　　　　　Collapse around us.

The Vine

I.

The yellow lawns smell dead in the long dry heat:
But in busy heaps
    the vine rears up again,
Impossible bulk
    profuse on every side,
Gaining in vital prevalence. How far
Do its deeper roots   feel down
For the unexhausted clouds
    of liquid   closely soaked
Under the beds and bricks, in the solid dark?

These sticky nights, I send out limbs
For the cooler reaches of the sheets,
With a feeling as though for the first time ever there.
Is this the best that I can find to meet
That pride of radical expectancy?

II.

Severed below, where the bark stuck out new green,
Between two trees above, one spanning limb
Darkening hangs with a dozen
        dead voluminous leaves
Gathered in drooping gobbets, brown and fat
As bats' bodies; a veined translucency
At the edges, in folds, against the light of the sky;
Like skinny wings. Shaken in each weak breeze,
The quivering of their tenuous
       and passive agitation
Is out of right proportion
To the weight these sleeping drops borrow from me.

A Willow

Last night, and this familiar willow tree
Secured in brain for a bit
            on account of this
Dropping lines, long articles, upward
Knottily   from the trap moon of the brook,
Tending toward its match, the one above,
    Tidily shining.

Green beneath daylight: this
        complexion of many curves
Without a rushing, tumbles;
Here, stiff basketry;
          there, radical strands
Upreaching: all a constituted structure—
Glossing, apparently, with a sight
Some servant or some tyrant contiguities
Which I can never know   to handle bare.

Do I begin to feel a hold?—
When nothing other than is fixed out there
Seems to be found
        according to
Whatever shapes or uses wait
On mutable powers at best presumed
To work in many a corner of my state.

What snags, and what against? It all
Speaks, I expect,
      in fluent metaphor
In some unlearnt, not unknown, dialect.

Heron Work

To be the breach itself
     in a distressing rest;
A blip, one spreading kiss
     pricking the long neat water,
A single instance of the river's life
Stirring at the level, fish's nose
Or dipping fly.

But there is heron work besides,
Worth its stress of duty; whose grave attention
Can outstrip, can bar such under-courses.

Heron, exemplary overseer, seeing,
Leaps to prevent with short, dramatic force,
Coming
     like hammers into dream
Down on the spiritual substance, quick:
Its sure opposition
A dark reunion.
Another whose apt method I must learn.

Heron Carriage

My old familiar comes overhead,
Bulk of a tidy hull,
        mass simply carried.

Breastbone with a sperm-whale curve
Is a grey ship's airborne bow,
Dips in a see-saw with the rigid legs
Out long,
        pace twice a quiet heart, light craft
On heaviest water
            in the steady
Function, operation of its flight:

Firm, confirming planes, a little like fans,
Machinery-like,
Just up, just down;
          so soberly heron
Rows across fen air
      with an even stroke,
No need of any

Sweeping to the rear:
      keeping
An even, strainless beat,
No sputtering, dive, or glide, as doves around,
Or wren-like fibrillation;
Goes in a big composure, as driven by gears:

Soberly heron works the tapered wings,
Lit from below,
        calm Icarus-person. One
Great urge
Of those, so slightly
        cranking, and so large;—
One long, embracing impulse over space
Athwart,—and it might surge
Away on that resisting emptiness.

Lilac or Buddleia

I didn't learn a single thing
About the lilac. Or is it a buddleia? But

When the other shrubs, and even the garden table,
Moved, they were moved in total lifelessness,
Stiff in the storm from the west;

While the hunks of pink
Lolling poodle above
(Since this—either lilac or buddleia—produces
Clumpy, irregular,
        not conical, sprays)
On the ends of long elastic and resilient
Branches
       were so lively in their great
Voluminous wagging.

At the lowest of the dependent points,
        on the arching, sunlit staves,
Hung vigorously down,
        one alongside
Its other, far out in the open air,
Two poodle chunks were bouncing around each other,

Meeting—as though for the happy interval
Before they must be called away, and the way
Has to be gone. I told you I was a mess.
Everything else was totally irrelevant.

Tropicbirds

Human faces
       pass so easily,
As tropicbirds I have seen between
Grey and green crags at shoulder height
With white Hawaiian falls
Falling
       to pools and the equable rivers:

Pale bodies   gliding,
Slow but at the swoop

Unforced,
       never darting,
       nor morose;
Ray-like—
       buoyed and waving;
Tails' long streamers
         tenuously trailing.

Encounters with the Fauna

Barely below the face,
                a glossy shape of leaf
Shows by its even glide the current
Otherwise unknown.
                Along the bank
I modify my step
To keep pace with it; then
It catches on the flow,
Bucks over and sinks away,
                out of sight. I go on,

Turning off the path, stepping up to a bridge's hump.
On the far side ahead,
An animated brownness over
                green, one deer's
Plump physique, twitches: a lustrous, supple
Density,
              head nosing over grass
In fluid but distinct meanders, like
A swan's ogival gestures when it slurps
The buoyant weed,
              and sharp little tapering legs,
Which in their repositioning seem to pluck,
As the machinery in play
Of a harpsichord, the tufty ground.

To think its apparition
Has nothing at all to do with the concurrent
Disappearance of the leaf,
Or with the deliberation of keeping
                    pace, or my sudden choice
To take this long way back,
Is questionably hard; it seems to have come
According to the laws of narrative
Moralised, the ordinance of
A mild Bunyanical process.

                    Next, however,
Another deer, its mate, comes into view.
The plain reality
            of each one to the other—
One with its miniature
                    horns, and the one
Without;—a sense of referent bearing now
Precluding me, comes home; while, down the lawn,
Come two exuberant humans.
                    I indicate
Coyly the wildlife;
            which escapes
In two or three bounds (twice) into a quailing
Hedge. . . .

                    This evening, mimic steps
Of impulse loop and run:
Swing of a snuffling nose, the lift
Of a cautious head, and the flourish of going away.
Some relatives for these present themselves.

What other furtive critters sneak
Demure or shifty in my habitat,
For which mundaner figures must be
Come upon, to bring them into view?

Not watchable, not
Fixable,

But moving with their proper sinuous sheen,
Delicate wobble of weight
In bushy tangles,—and the keen
Tickle their lively feet
                    make on our tender linings?

On Nature

'I am caught between delight and "come off it" at times, when
faced with the natural world as mediated through Wong . . .'

A lady who saw me last as a little boy
Sent me a birthday card last year, which read:
'We thought you might enjoy
This strange sea creature'. Was it a dugong?
Could it perhaps have been a manatee
(Backed like a walrus, yet lacking the two-prong
Dental motif of that stirring pinniped),
The animal that moved me in the green
Serenity of that painted submarine
Landscape, as in a Wong-tormented sea—
Aquatic life 'as mediated through Wong'?
    I did enjoy it. Is it all vanity,
And nothing for it, to associate
Sentiments frankly owned appropriate
To human persons or 'humanity'
With a dugong or perhaps a manatee,
In openness to unobvious relation?
    The accosting form we know we don't create
Is strange to us still, in status (say, in state):
Form into which, with dilection and surprise,
Inside the pale of impotent speculation,
One might, in a tender fantasy, project
Some ultramarine and humanlike supplies—
Transmitted while we try to harmonize,
In exuberant theoretical temptation,
Subject and object, subject and subject.

Castigation (I)

Must you adulterate all the most really other
    Of your discovered things?—proud to possess,
Dandle and tame them: always to adorn
    That sweet creation, *summum bonum*, you?—
Redecorating with so many shells
    That luscious, extrovert urbanity.

With languid finish, you reel off the list:
    These rarities, ordained your cloudy creatures.
By virtue of that stock (your timid brag),
    With brisk allure, you, carefully triumphant,
Claim admiration,—when it should cast out
    From self to uncertain things; begin with you:

Attention blowing into what you realize—
    To take thus, with a kind prerogative,
The perfumes and the figures they dispense;
    Not just to enrich, however, that complexion—
A proud bird weaving scraps of borrowed string
    Into its nest, mistaking nest for self.

Fanciful nature (foreign, full of fancy),
    And histories, and building into form:
All wild with mind, as well as strange to us
    In execution of ancient sovereign process:
Thorny with hieroglyphics, they make terms
    By contrast and obscure comparison.

Changing effect, all; but the presence, *there*—
    Standing constant, feral, in the shake,
Or shaking through ostensible repose.

Dealt either way, in justice of equation,
Accordant similes play to expand
  Our gardens—what they realize to embrace:

Scripture of webs, and luxuries of design;
  Ways in the shade; the compassing of meadows;
And creatures who divide their tendencies
  With us. So goblins, without manners, fling
Dark missives at us—down from our human rooves,
  It seems; or out of common garden bushes.

Castigation (II)

Daily, with some historical setbacks,
For all these years I have been nudging slowly
Out of my stupid nature—

An outward transit, never

Emergence. Swivelling back
From time to time
        to a prospect of the waste,—
The mortifying mammocks of indiscretion
Gummy and gross, in a fraudulent perspective,
Far and very close,—
      The sage eye, in a push
           for self-collection, scans it,

All of it, from above; and the floating wrecks,
Officially derelict
          and craftily without haste,
Rock behind in their dubious repose,
Suggesting 'better', though something, has never yet
Been good enough.

I may be coolly brushing my teeth one day,
And when I stoop, left hand pressed to the wet
Enamel   rough with old, re-moistened paste,
Its arm a rigid column, and my head,
Canting into a more convenient tilt,

Some view that ought to have been always clear
Dislodges, in a glimpse from underneath
The stiff upholstery
              of mental disposition:

The meaning of a signal,
                  in misperception of which
I was the disappointment to one who since
Has seemed a disappointment slung on me.

Or, on the busy train,
                  the carriage shocks: and I see
How, as I crossed them, all those bridges burned
Behind me   that I later tried to find;

And I can tell how in the lapse
From which I even now hope to recover,
Those lost companions, laden
                  with too much inferent feeling, learned—
In the sight of narrow space
                  widening in between
My back, perhaps still amiable, and them—
That other people they could know need not
Be quite as tiresome as I had been.

Castigation (III)

To conscience it can come as no surprise.
But the reflective mind, when it occurs,
Is out of service, and no rallying
Of mortifying habits is enough.

The reinforcements, jolted into work,
The whole machine of introspective caution:
Vain. Admit, reactively, the sad
Familiar taste of a returned dislike.

But can you muster *relish*? Either way,
Some stupid sense of undesert remains.
Do you catch yourself expecting to have charmed?

Avoid, at least, that irritating sin
Of asking your acquaintances to share
The shock, as if it were a true enigma.

Castigation (IV)

How do they feel the slide?—is the course well known
Of that mundane and necessary marvel,
Leaving its evidence, never caught at the instant,

How face and finish age ahead of them
Endangered as they wait to be happy again
And muse: against whom, whom only, has each one sinned?

Some cruel or tender notes get stuck inside
Close inches of so many tacit throats;
Recalcitrant in the long red streets at night.

They kiss together, and part, as it were, together,
Heading for unlike comforts (it is implied),
And cannot ever stroke the dead friend away.

Paper Burning

After its several days pressed in a book
The envelope lay all morning on the table.
Taken outside, it burns in a gentle wind
On the mossy ground.

Six pages written, folded up in thirds,
Are tenderly exhibited in turn.
One by one, the sheet above each new sheet
Peels dead lively away,
The words too legible, yellowing first and browning.

Zones of black wash over them like the
Shifting colours of octopus rind, a
Thin pink borderline
        the bright confine
Of all the spreading grey that grows alive,
Makes puppetry of the paper; till the mass
Blooms apart
        as boiling sugar—
Flowers rotting out wide,
        and falling away;
Subsides into its very dead
Tenuity at the margin; lava-flow

Curls the next page
        to a fruiting foam
With plastic, self-exhausting energy;
And one more gleaming tract of what I said
Goes for a moment foxed with livid,
Liquid, cancerous patches, leaving
Nothing left to be delivered now.

A story comes to mind
        about the Hawaiian chiefess
Ka'ahumanu, the king's most favoured wife,
Who, far out on a heavy board in the surf,
Turned to the shore among
        the fluctuant assembly
And found, where the smoke went up
        with its narrow streak diffusing,
The high place, picked out on the brunted
Cone-slopes of Le'ahi, Diamond Head,

Knowing it marked the spot where under guard
In the precinct, left to nature, was retained
The strangled flesh
        of the beau she had chosen,
Had not been allowed.

The Wai'anae Range

The road from Wahiawā to the north and home
Runs alongside the Wai'anae range,
And when, for these sixteen years, slid over,
I left it half-way across the world,
Waialua cane, I thought,
      for the fine Waialua sugar,
Cane shaken to waves or bristled in wind,
Went green across even plains that lay
Between the road and the Wai'anae range;—

Though in truth some years had passed, myself so near,
Still passing down that road, running the eye
Over the sugarless land,—with the lapse unknown;
Change in the green and the brown
Which ought to have come home, ought
      to have mattered more.

From Wahiawā to the northern shore
There are no fires lighted over the plains
To clear the leaf, and to make the cut cane's
Liquor run freer;
      the fields have outlasted labour,
Lived out demand; and the flapping cane's
Cover   rolls only in the vain
Journeys made over the distant years
To the long road home
      and the Wai'anae range
And the rise on the road where ahead the ocean appears.

How to count everything lost
        for the price of that sugar?
Then, late, another loss with the last cane haul.

And there was the Pacific,
        and there was no more cane,
Cane the small child had known, and the adolescent
Never felt go out; more gone,
        more really, for the years
Far off: flat gone, at my one, now past, return

To that stretch of road where, long to the west,
The ridges and peaks of the Wai'anae range
Define on the sunset horizon a supine
Figure,—since missed,
        or always too much missed,—

Clearer now than when the child,
Living near, knew what to see,
Not how:
        the pregnant woman lying down,
Mist over the belly—the jagged breast
Turgid, legs lain out at rest
Shoreward, athwart
        the sun's day-long
Scrutiny making gradual shade
On the green
        contours, the creasing-down
Of a rampart face:
        shades definite, or dissolved
In the splintered lights of her atmosphere of rain;—

Changeless substrate under that changeable
Sky, as if she had slept between,
Over the sugarcane
          and the vacant fields:
This carrying, still unmoving mother,
Woman-with-child of the Waiʻanae range.

Giant waters'
          far-fetched waves,
Broken on coral teeth—catching unseen—
Or broken harder on Waialua shores,
Pounded,
          affronting,
Sounded
          deep inland:
Ran

Piercing, as if it were a feral boar's
Grunts, old songs
Say in their live
Fragments; northern uproar
Mistaken for the human noise
Of Wahiawā,
          its bruit of a royal birth
Beaten from its pale of mothering stones
Spread in the sight of the dome, the girth,
Limpet-like,
          of that folkloric childbed:

Curving Kaʻala's sinuous, strange,
Enclosing, clouded
        womb that never bore:
Now with its small, white globe-antenna poised
Above the navel,
        tracer of satellites,
On the brimming crest, the arx, of that gravid home,
The swelling store filled out to that arching line
Long and high
        on the Waiʻanae range.

Mist of Ka'ala

after the Hawaiian: a paraphrase

Listen, drifting mist above Ka'ala,
Carried on the Mālua,
      the wind of the land:

Don't stir yourself
      with too much haste
Into quiet waters: hold, for the wind
To settle down to quiet.

There's something, a disquiet, chafes at me;
The fresh northwesterly wind, the Kiu wind,
Penetrates my skin,
      shivering
Thighbones, thrumming deep
      to the innermost rib.

And do not stir yourself with too much haste
Into quiet waters; wait
For the wind to come, when it will, to quiet.

Would you ever believe the sweet voice of the land-shells,
Softly singing
      through the quiet night
In the late, late midnight hours?

But do not stir yourself with too much haste
Into quiet waters lying at peace;
Linger until the wind has come to quiet.

Two Passages from Janus Secundus (1511–1536)

I.

How could I
        bear Jove
As rival in
        my love?

My eyes can't even bear
My own lips' rivalry

When they linger
        over your face,
        too close to see.

II.

Like the colour the rose
Made wet with the long night's dew
Spreads
        in the purple dawn,
Those lips are red by morning, wet
With kisses of the long night, still renewed.

Around that darker mouth,
As snowfall   undisturbed, her face
Lies and rises; like
A wreath in complement:

As when a girl
Cups a violet
In one pale hand;

Or the way the new cherry shines
Beneath the late-flowering blossom
When the tree has its summer and spring at the same time.

Why, when you join the most burning of all kisses,
Do I have to leave your bed?   At least
Save on your lips this red—
Until the opacity of noiseless night
Leads me back to your side.

But if meanwhile they sample
Some other person's kiss,
Let the colour wash right out of them, as the blood
Dims in my draining face.

In the Lower Church of S. Ponziano, Spoleto

I.

A composite capital, of Roman make,
Lends itself in the lower church to a strange
Repurposing: as a plinth or pedestal.
Whether it was by practical device
Or deviant impulse hauled
Down, inverse, into a small
Quadrangular depression in the floor,
It is no idiomatic syntax, this
Attaching and diverting upset, its
Secure, preposterous new consolidation.

A column from
This basis—neat
In glossy polish,
Of darker stone:
A marine mottle
(Purple and grey
Green)—ascends
Clean, debonair,
Into the dampish
Air of this Crypt;
The whole bizarre
Projected member
Having the look of
A weird, visionary
Pachyderm part: a
Scriptural monster
Blithely implanting
By the altar its foot,
All shaggy with rigid
Curls underneath the
Slender cylinder of its
Towering elephant leg:
Floor-stones compacted thus into that shallow recess.
Or, from an old woody base of crotchety stems
(The pagan head and broken wreath around,
Severed, replanted into the buxom dip)
Springs—with elastic push—the young dark shoot,
The new year's growth, right up to adjoin the vault:
As though the head spilled   fresh and invisible roots   down under the flagstones.

II.

⊓⊓⊓⊓⊓⊓⊓⊓⊓⊓⊓⊓⊓⊓⊓⊓⊓
THAT THE PAIR NEARBY
OF ANGULAR SHAFTS,
WANTING
THEIR
Tips,
Tapered
Each to its
Own petite
Canonically-
Sited capital
Shouldn't be
Regarded as a
Mason's whim
Or a foppery of
Design, but sign
Of a resourceful,
Economical mind
For structure, and,
Incidentally, also a
Thrift in ornament;
A 'collage' (whether
Or not we impute as
Curious impulse any
Antiquarian fancy for
Process and provenance):
All is casually explained by
The guide's avowal that in a former state
They served as markers, mêtae, in a Roman
Chariot circus. Imagine; scudding over the sand,

Sidelong the wheels flung round these terminal staves:
Raced to obtain no 'incorruptible crown'.
Then here they come, brought into a dark subjection;
Dug up, and set up, recondite—sustaining
The newly spreading vault, closed low, near overhead.
⊔⊔⊔⊔⊔⊔⊔⊔⊔⊔⊔⊔⊔⊔⊔⊔⊔⊔⊔⊔⊔⊔⊔⊔⊔⊔

A Letter of Advice

As Jung says, sound advice does little mischief:
Everyone ignores it. Mine
Is likelier unsound;
                 and who can say
How dangerous that could be? I have been at times
Persuasive.

       If you will carry on wishing aloud
For somebody to tell you what to do,
Some weak, well-wishing soul—allow not me,
Aminta—may
         throw policy to the wind
And buckle in the end.

Take it for admonition, the above,
And what succeeds
As an overheard diversion of no weight.

           *

Isle of Aminta,
        long remain
Atoll of fight,
         dry land presuming up—

Withstanding provocation,
       ever again,
Of a pious, smug Pacific. Long impede
Its reasonable billows.

Ruck up your reefs around,
                        get a bit of surf going;
Have it show its teeth as it near your bays, lagoons,
The beetling cliffs.

                        *

Yours the straw hat of generous size,
Why the hell not?
                        Be it ductile and bestuck:
Feathers of cuckoo, grebe and green
Woodpecker;
                        snazzy ribbon—
Coral, puce or plum:
                        may it lend killing

Blandeur (let me have it) to your bloody
Flash-floods of obscenity and bust-up.
Trample it into the crumpled daisies
                        and
The dandelions inappropriately.—

                        A band
Of hired ruffians in livery
Tumble together (may they) at the
Sounding of your whistle—sprung
From obvious hiding in the floral borders:
Emotional banditti, not without
Moral motivations.

And you eftsoonz,
Reverting
        to a lustrous camel cloche,
Continue pruning, peaceable once again
In a scene of grotesque havoc as if by Bosch;
All kinds of crazy shit—a validation
Of domesticity; tinted   foil to that streak.

                    *

I do admire the genial sanity
Of your impatient, tempered dignities;
The cavalier sobriety with which
You package up—
            unswaddle now and then—
With sensitive vigour
                    and no cocktail spilt,
Contrarian shitstorms of primeval aggression
(Measure of your manifest,
                sure instinct for the real) and eke
Those intermittent versions of tendresse—

Your sober intimations of a sane
Containment, with a country singer's ease,—
A belied, a belying
            and still candid ease:
Irony, pathos, honky-tonk relief;
The deadpan fatalism, the understated
Overstatements: always coolly in tune
Or thereabouts.

                    *

The more trickles you dam,
The more the open course runs out with a look
Of meaning it.
               But, after all, why foreclose
On possibilities   which are not quite
Recourses—
               beaver up those varying channels?
Is it nothing
               to be committed faithfully
To possible chance, to omission
                              of commitment
To the sealing of gutters, the higher raising, coating,
Smoothing, of narrow banks?

                    * * *

                    . . . . Why do I want
Lone islands all
               of valuable selves?—
Remote, with traffic overseas unknown
To me, for whom a little
                    harbour is laid out calm.
Why break up my defences facing each,

Hoping the same materials may serve
The other's need—
               a neighbour-island need,
Suggested—fortify
                    their shores on other sides?

Sentiment

From some romantic fleet under the clouds—
From light unseen flotillas
              answering to your doubt,
Reposing on miles of wide, indefinite blue;—

Assembled of conditions, caveats,
Savvy demands in winsome planning;
          bearing
Cannon sleeping still, in a dreaming pause
Of your still silent play
              with revolution and war;—

From those flotillas lurking far offshore,
Conveyed along a soft shudder of wind,
Perhaps a cordial sound, like a proud whoop,
Fanned over, on occasion, to your ear,
To ruffle and caress you.

But here, half-open worry
              bit all your fingers red.

Modification

A whale in shadow passes underneath
My tiny keel. In its approximate mass,
Presence in deeper shade, I half divine
The accidental threat of a large indifference.

With nothing understood,
Something is undergone
By the floating vessel.

See the slow-quivering beak, overwhistled in wind,
Give up presuming. Lines are allowed to run;
Lures are forgotten. Woody knocks resound
About my chest. Was there even a gentle swell?

Above Water

What is the appeal of these
                    disarranging arrangements?
Like moiré silk or tortoise-shell,
Made of the upcast light and lucent shade
Reflected from the water to the wall
Or bridge's undercurve, in cursive lines:—

Slack-tied nets dissolving;
            scales, or the skeleton jaws
                        of fish, in flamboyant change.

Is it the transference to stone or brick
(Not dumb, but muted by
                    habitual passing contact)
Of the always vanishing continuity
And movingness of water, evoking life?
Or is it the gift to water's running face
Of stationary character, the wall's
Standingness: matter the mind regards,
There in its volatile enlivenment,
More consciously than it does
                    the cinema's screen; which lends
To its animate and water-forming light
A portion of its palpable resistance—

Body participant
            with these unbodily things:
                        an image of physique?

The disc of a phonographic record gives
A bulky reference to its phantom cargo:
Source the incorporate mind can realize
As the dark circle turns, and the sash of light
Swells in a breathing billow
                across the roughened bands,—
Where fingers small enough
                might feel the ridges of pitch
From which, as an illusion of memory,
The spectral voice emerges.

Crackle and hiss, faint cycles of the belt,
Bring to the mental office treating touch
This welcome memorandum of fixed impression,

Over which the human
        Monument (cenotaph),
                as though re-living, surges,—

Like fissures interrupting even space
Over which, on the wall, with slight distortion,
The water-figures in this luminous guise
Slide with no shade of notice:
                glossily irrespective.

Water as light: less tangible than water;
Abstraction, or a second self; refined
And rarefied, existing to the mind
As a glancing flash on the wavelet only, until
Now visibly salient, spread
                on the intercepting plane's
Stability, where motion is arrested,
While on its front this moving supervenes:
Tiger-stripes, or the dark dyes of a shrimp;

Or as the wind overturning
        grass in ripple-strands

Waves; or the leaf-stained dapple
        of tree-light, when the boughs
                sway fugally back and forth.

Into the brick or stone of the water-light
No pebble can be dropped: there is no depth,
But only unobscuring shadow there,
And out of its face no dark fish will project.

At the Clunch Pit Alone

(*Orwell, Cambs.*)

Grass abraded
      down to the chalk, white ways
Radiate, branching, from the quarry's bowl—
Lines of foam,
      waves' edges, crossing
Sea-like contours, silver figures rubbing
Out of the verdigris of a Celtic stater,
Cupped—
      seen from the highest ledge

Around the vital now and flexing crater
In solar
      throwing-down: the sudden

Blowing of a light-stain—fast for a growing;
A flash but slowed, coquettishly morose—

Spots of glare
On white and green,
Fading, diving under, as they rush
Over the unseen troughs, uneven rises,
Quickened by a wind
      brawny on harried cloud.

The rubble dust flew up the white lap, let loose
At the lip, in a spray on bare skin, spattering glasses;
Sea-like—as on rocks, or a harbour
                    wall; another sweeping
Gust. And nothing surely could pollute
For long this open
Lap in a landscape
Otherwise so flat,
                    the unsubjective
Wind being always at its curves;
It must be the cleanest place for miles and miles.

These Foolish Things

That icy mind of prose. It is often you;
It is seldom me—
          and scarcely ever I—
And then for a moment only—
And only in a rallying to protect
Its antithetical dependency;
                    Confronting cool with cool—
With a snapping logic stung into offence
By rhetoric hard as yours may seem to me.

These foolish things prosper in narrow crannies
Sheltered in part
          from the puffing of life outside.
They fumble into themselves—
They are fumbled so by a will not wholly fast
In shame, to elude, precariously at best,
                    Whatever is gross and chills—
All that offends in that expedient, dull
Stupor supposing this may not be that.

Hwasong

Out of the orange smoke, the carapace,
Immaculate in white, slides up the unseen
Cylinder over the blasting of its skirt.
And will this flight, the latest of the long
Succession of fired temptations, make amends
For earlier failures of the ambitious aim?

A symbolist ballet of gleaming things
Careering into the waste of realism:
The glossy towers, the reassuring points,
Ferry my dummy warheads into bits.
The water shall be blown out of the water.
Play it again. Or play another song.

Oh, but the gentle machines, the unnerving plop.
Is every launch a necessary dud:
Ballistic recompense, inside itself
Hauling its ghostly substitute for mark?
They sink my effigies in broken water,
Retracting nothing to the eager State.

Summer 2017

Motivations

I.

Not a receptacle, since not,
As such, to be relied upon.
A conduit for matter as thought?—
Or reflex, with the fixative
Somewhere outside one: volatile things
Replaced, so one can walk away,
Later return, and find them safe,
Reformed in combinations, and
In paraphrases of themselves;
Put back more sympathetic, more
Interresponsive with the shapes
And kinships of ideas (such
As they are) at home: and turned around
In terms appropriate to one's
Own leaky tin. The fear of not
Being able to hold on to things;
Though models may be made and stored—
Not quite the thing, but your thing-thing
Still waiting when you look again.
The fear of never being a thing
To hold or figure;—yet one must
Mirror with trouble, and may take care
The arresting agent fixes down
The models with all phantom freaks.

II.

Not a low service to what stood
Before it, past the coast of it.
Rather, affectionate, maculate
But fair administration, whether
Tenderly hard or soft, of what
The fabrication offers, in
A mood of deference to both
The matter in specific, and
In general the whole domain
Of weighted specificities
It represents, or recreates.
So what inheres, lies in the make,
Is what was fated to be in
The making; ran across the way,
Suggesting a formation with
What else lay round it or prepared
Its path. By grades the outer world
Comes into view, unpresupposed
In character, made out but not
Created; and the prospect castigates.

III.

Convergence of two rivers, which contrast
The colours of their silt from two directions.
The water and its cargo slide away,
Down a third channel, and are lost. But here
Remains the roiling point of mixture, still
Detained in place by force from either side,
So in that wavering fixity persist
The fluid revolutions made in meeting.

Watching Snow

Turning again to the window, I find that, just in the minute
   Past, the whole space, which had made no appeal,
   Has filled with unanticipated snow.
Moisture caught up in the air, without   stress of presence beforehand,
   An unremarkable element unremarked,
Takes another form of its various person,
   As though embodied. Now the court is white,
Thick with a tenuous, copious vision of volume;
Fresh for its change to a sight; lavish supply
   Of object, turned attractively opaque;
Ponderability offered (if lusory always),
   Which by engaging calls up likenesses.

Poetry also   puts out from commonplace backgrounds—
   The atmospheres of thinking and of speech—
Stimulant shapes
   And clumps: the ordinary seems to fall
Into an order,
Fixed at a moment when all its bidding address lies
   Poised and suggestive, winningly arranged,
   Arrestingly, and the words have weight as things.

Why should it not revert to such
Moments of sudden symbolic purchase—not always
   'Insight'; a mere fortuitous apprehension
Somehow accruing
Weight of significance—nothing specially meaning,
   And nothing specially meant, follow what may?
Often it issues

Out of the inarticulate fronts of things
Only by chance acknowledged, or tacitly guided
   By the un-rhetorical persuasions of
   Quick weather, weather timed to catch a mood—
Changes in light, or the instantaneous prospect:
Unexplained trick of coherence, which, as it passes,
Brings a thing up to us, holding it up to the outlet:
Newly estranging, affining;—
Holding us up in its way, which was ours;   I am brought up
Short, or resisted.

Now, on the stone of the outer sill of the window,
   The clumps dissolve in seconds. Some of them
Gather for longer on leaves.

On the Grasshopper in my Fennel

Slowly giving,
And with a releasing
Green-douce waft in the bending, more again
The lunglike fennel swells:

More velvet, caterpillar finials
Undo their richer fuzz
            to lacier plumes,
Elastic—
            between vigour and lassé
Greenery gesture,—
            fanned against
Displacements of the budging air:

All parts in motion at once;   as like
Harmony as not.
                    And the single, proud,
Fennel-coloured
Grasshopper—
            or bush-
Cricket it may be—
                        sprung

At the centre of its scented featherwork,
Aloof:

The perfect ego,   throned,
Open
        amid its easy
Flexible
Frondage

Organ—
        fennel nerves
Branching;
        fennel thoughts, a fennel creature—

Perches, every day,
        the jointed legs acute,
In simple, unimperious command,
Swaying.

Notes Toward a Fantasy

Naked impostors, we collect ourselves,
Summoned to the high place
      by our solemn headsman.

We are only from one division of the whole,
Single fey earth
      of many that must fall
As a let-loose pearl
           in a whole sea's play—a bead's
Weight in the scale,
      from the hidden point
Of prime agreement of all contrary sources,
Into our naked impostures.

Our own witnesses, weaving
Evidence
      of themselves
(Contrived as any case),
Uneasily conclude, living head-down
In gauzy letters that do not rise into substance.

(Could I undress the sentences, with such
A hand as this I use
      to dress remains!—)

He has applied a warm
        sunshine to grief,
And offers up sweet dying fruit
To any fly that creeps there unsuspicious.

Make up the unburied heads, and the skulls
Would sing in the wind, a whistling heap on the sea-cliff.

Assisi: After D'Annunzio

Assisi, in your deep peace my soul,
Turned inside, always, towards her own ends, never
Slackened; it clung to an image of your river
As when, on its grating bed, rough currents roll.

The river contorts, thirsty and blank
In the rage of a thirsting, pale desire.
Like flames that pant to shoot only ever higher,
The olive trees rear up from its twisted bank.

From above I saw it, far down, foaming in white.
I watched in the calm breath of the evening prayer
The tortive fervency of that pouring flood.

And the body of Francis, set alight
By the demon of flesh: I saw that also there,
Catching on spines of roses, spilling blood.

Shame, Shame, Shame

The Blunderhound is at the gate again,
Slopping my face in lurid effigy,
Drags the dull decoy, wax smearing his teeth:—
Out of his hole again. Rectitude, care,
And castigation;—I have betrayed the end,
And everything betrays me (as the Poet
Saith). The moping angels flood the lines,
Demanding revolution in my lands.

Drop the receiver. I have dark employment.
Shame is a tangle—evil botany there—
And stupidly embedded there you curl.
How many springs come back the plump weed that toys
At your fat pride? Pretentious Miseryguts,
Who does he think will care? *He* cares. The foot
Slips, and the traps convulse, and they rejoice
Greatly—the mumbling angels, and that dog.

The crimes are murmuring ferns in crevices;
Every mistake a noisy closet sin
In part divulged. (To whom?) A treachery,
A want of diligence, discoverable,—
And no duress to excuse collaboration.
God must be made to work mysteriously
If to forgive ourselves on our behalf
Is plausibly to be among his functions.

Now any lapse, in which attentiveness
To alien things accosted takes away
The weight,—beguiles the brain from its dull brood
Of needy suppliants requiring dues

That cannot now be rendered,—soon or late
Breaks up in some new striking-home of debt:
Debt to the Tutelaries, Messengers,
The velvet swarm around the muffled tower.

Soft for a time, again they glint out sharp,
The hard light glancing on the reptile sides:
The lucid choppers buzzing close again.
A raid at dawn on the suburban house
Of self-forgotten criminality:
Crime with a fine demeanour, day to day
Fooling itself. Outside, unseen, the vans,
The guns and visors. Crowds, gather and snap.

Imaginary they may be, not unreal,
The muttering furies. You solicited
Industrious response, with frozen studies;
Knitting up your covenant with words
In words, against the obdurate unfair.
Still they demand the benefit of doubt,
These island-crazy stammerings, caught short
Like water-flows caught sideways into ice.

Terms and Conditions

I.

Because the inevitable circumstance
Clings to it, and because its dares require
An answer, I resist—until, detached
From the redundant scene, each thing appears
More as it is: the pressures of the time
That prove or test affiliation, and give
Offence or flatter, floating out the baits
Of provocation and pleasure, and so define
(The worse served up, our sentiment served the better),—
Relax, or pull towards a history
Put in its place: no need to ingratiate;
No longer selling its endeared demands
On manufacture of identities
That coax with newly-evolved taxonomies.

II.

Better indulge the current, judge remains
Severely, by contemporary sense,
Or to indulge the dead, taking their claim
Across the interval as reassuring?
Are they, in fact, the purest elements,
Refined, are found the most tenacious—all
Ephemeral coercions of the day
Dispersed with buffering nights? Or is it only
Pride, too stubborn, lofty, will not pay
The debt till one can keep a foot outside,
(Capricious punters having moved away),
When no one makes a profit by it but
Oneself;—gratuities, royalties, gladly paid
Only to have-beens, or their sprightly shades?

Plague-Year Epistle

Ah, Stacey, Stacey, it's the same old thing,
Fens of Despond—
            any place a Red River Valley;
The moth and the rust—and mainly the moth;
Mould on the windows, around the
                    sink. . . . the leak in the skylight.
Flies in the kitchen bins again;
Aphids, powdery mildew, in the garden.
Rats at the birdseed.

And in the canes
We kept inside,
                to prop
Later the over-reaching stalks
Outside,—woodworm,   uphoarding pyramids
Of bamboo slag, like sand in the lower cone
Of a timer. That's a new one. Same old thing.

'Earning minor ducats in a thankless job',
With snivellers and
            the imperviously content;
Continual onslaughts of pernicious dickheads,
Quivering, oleaginous priglets,
Simpering tuft-hunters.
                By your leave,
Sometimes I feel provocative, McDowell.
But nobody seems provoked—only a bit
Put off;   at best, put out.

And everyone so 'ground-
                breaking' indeed,
You can hardly move for all the muddy ditches.
Bit of a Roman teapot?—better look
            busy with them mattocks, bitches.
Roll out the tarpaulins. Give it over.

Holes, and holes; and harrowing small-talk,
Bores and their big-talk:
                look you, there's nothing for it.
'Playes with the dug
                though finds no comfort ther',—
Be a lamb and agree.

                .... There are pets among the flock;
Mm, yes—would I unloose these? But as for that,
It's less o' the 'violent imaginative puberty',
More *Buy Your Own Canoe*, and the gentle art
Of canny drifting—
                bumping along downstream
To the Camelots of their glittering
Careers.
            So much for 'the groves of Academe'.

Meanwhile the brisket in the fridge
Goes bad, no matter how much salt you rub in it.

Is it just a seasonal dream,
Or are my correspondents really,
Some of them, readier now to acquiesce
In disconcerting happiness? So it seems.
Can this be *honourable*?
                .... Look here, old man,
It baulks imagination, no?

Seinfeld, sex, and a second glass of wine?—
So far, so good, but only if followed up
By a really decent lunch;
Three courses, wine—all French;—
And even then it's a coasting afternoon
Of indigestion, lassitude and guilt.

Fuck it, McDowell, it's all the moth and the rust
And the Red River Valley—
                especially as sung by
Stevie Nicks and 'some handsome dude', as a dear and
Dormant friend once said. At the time of writing,
Nevertheless, there are many people living
Who have no list of grievances
                against me; and at least
One of them is Stevie;
                and of the rest,
I hope I am not unjustified in believing
That some of them   may even be known to me.

Ah, Stacey, Stacey, it's no use; more and more
The balls of paper glide, without
Resistance,
                crumpled neatly and well-aimed,
Into the crater,
                messages into the void.
And what could be
                the best outcome—that it should one day
Blow its cone right off? It makes me want
To break things. I'm upset by broken things.

Ah Stacey, *ça suffit*. What cheer with you?

Trifle to O

O dear, it may be   that our lives
       touch only at one or two points.
Either can dilate, contract,
Dear O,
      can try to superimpose:
There is no concentricity,
No contact till the circles roll, and the points

Meet—our perimeters
Calibrate;

There only   are the overlaps;

And it seems, when it comes, so easy, as though
It had always been
      within reach—just sat in your lap, O,
Or under your chapeau.

When the orbs align, when the twin dials turn
Each to the final digit it wants,
And both click with their codes at once,
And your safe opens,
        and my adjacent safe,
O O, how reassuring—
       albeit, or more
Peculiarly, as we make an unusual duo.

And I'm not prepared to say that in me there's no
Run-out-of-town rogue element, lying low,
Stricken, morose, immonde,
Glad of a passage to your
                    off-kilter round,
                    your faerie lond,
For a wash and a shave and a change of clothes
And a convivial brew, O.

Fancypiece (II)

I fear to think what gods may haunt these newly
Rediscovered territories of mine.
At my desk I slouch. Far off, in that Ultima Thule,
In the clumsy figures of a wayside shrine
Lost and found in the waste, I recognise
My own hands' work; and offer my dulia duly;
And swivel, heels in the snow—training my eyes
Back on the wavering, rough, unruly line
Of my incautious boot-marks. It was unwise
To come so far. To anticipate mishap,
Better add no more than a monster to the map.

Song of My Peas

My peas
        are coming up roses,
But I really felt
        like peas.

There's a goose
        in a tin of its own fat
        in the cellar,
In dark congealment,
        waiting for those peas.

My peas are coming up
        roses, only roses.
I suppose
        I'm getting used to it by degrees.

Roses are pleasing.
        It is their season.
But now a pod of peas
        would please me more.

My peas are coming up roses.
        Son of a whore.
I knelt in the dirt,
        in the rain,
        and I planted peas.

Ferrets

May your ferret be of no fatter girth
Than the fattest rabbit that scampers in the caverns.
Pity the ferret that finds itself more fat
Than the rabbit that is most fat of the tunnelling den.

Have a care for the girth of any adventuresome beast,
That it hath no larger girth
Than the fattest coney of the band that scoops
In the warren of thy desires.

Micro-Adjustment

Why should I chain the Mammoth? It would still
Heave and reel in the cobwebs, and exist!

Tumbles in the Slough

When I think too much of what I have seen and heard,
News or opinion, conversation at table,
A stray uncivil, or even a civil word,
That will do it.

And when I think of a thing I've done,
The doing of it caught abroad,
Recorded, somewhere set;—
When I remember what I have said that sticks;
Any time I am made for a space not to forget:
That will do it.

Further, when I turn to the inward hoard
Of never wholly known ideas
To which the bare committed facts,
Betraying shadow-parts, can only be
Corrupt relata, and the vision clears
Appallingly in the murk down there—
The litter of still-coherent wrecks
The covering sands leave, fitfully, partly bare
(Since no wreck ever can
                    be a perfect write-off:
Ungentle days unsettle it),—that will do it.

Or you, in affection, venture to make light of
An old mistake: and when you do, and I veer
And slip between the behind and the dark ahead,
That does it.

. . . One thing I think I know, if it may be said;
One simple rule, of which,
                    at times, I am almost sure.
Most people I have known—none to be named—
Should almost certainly be more,
And certainly not less, ashamed.

The Drains in This House

I shall put some red ruge on my face said Ethel because I am
very pale owing to the drains in this house.

Ashford, *The Young Visiters*

Not only what we have run today
Stands in the sink and will not drain away,
But richer liquors from below
Spill out a deepening, wide, mephitic slough
Over the garden, just beneath
The back door's tread, floating a wreath
Of pale, revolving scum I fear to find
Has left behind
A blight of yellow scurf
When the uncouth pool sinks down again to the sewer.
Discarded powerless by receding surf,

With what dark aim, and by what lure,
Came the fat staring masses on the shore,
Immobile, ostentatious, which
Were not washed up but *swam* toward the beach
In droves?—but driven by what planned
Or hoped-for thing, onto the strand
That seemed to rise beneath them? Can I guess
What stubbornness,
What period's fatal turn,
What unacknowledged purpose brought them here?
What can the cranky lighthouse-keeper learn

Of all those secret agents that appear
(If they appear) and dive again
Too rapidly to know? Some prickling spear.
That curious periscope.

What narwhals and what U-boats can explain,
                    Each by its separate trope
             Of feral will or furtive pain,
Neglected guilt or acrobatic hope,
                    Each by the wish or whip
That moves it, and the courses it has steered,
The finer problems of the general weird
One drees half in surprise, seeing it unfold?
                    What can one tell of the nearly quiet drip?

Among what nesting moths and creeping mould
             Gather those drops? Along what runs
And hidden ledges have they seeped or rolled;
                    Into, or onto, what
Surface, or cavity, do they plummet—heard once,
                    Then lost again (though not
             Cast out of mind) in cavernous funds
With secret sources,—threatening the rot
                    That gives them away too late?
Among what rocks and wrecks, and submarine
Cables ferrying what unguessed, unseen
Informations, and what silent speeches,
                    Over the unsurveyed beds of a strait

Forgotten in between two charted beaches
(My old familiar resorts):—down in that dark,
             What fish are fretting in my sea?—
Enquiring at the woodwork of what ark
Of mine?—in the effluent waste of what factory,
                    Also of mine?
             And what nets, or what line
Can bring them up; and what revolting features
(Members excrescent, menacing tusk or spine)
                    Might anglers find who take

Their chances in such waters, and won't dock,
              Won't head back to the warm, until they break

The stubbornness of chance, and feel their shock?
Are we banked in, all round, with an ancient, great,
          Disgracefully inefficient dyke
The shape of a consciousness, with a small flood-gate
Cut here and there? Is our fabric something like
              A huge and un-
              Suspected marble run?
Or like a fancy complication clock—
Perhaps a very labyrinthine one;—
              All aqueducts, and sluices,
And conduits on tipping arms that balance
              Each its own basin;—one drop more and it loses

All of its burden at once? Do these restless gallons
Trickle, and plunge, and gurgle inside my walls,
          Under the floors, in the attics, by
The unimaginable protocols
Of works, to conceive which is to mystify?
          And have I misbelieved for years
          The run-off had escaped away
That wells and muddles with the rain today,
          In its dilution still dilating
              Over new frontiers?
And everything brought up and circulating
Over the blockage, under the stress of rain:
          Where does it go, when the channel clears,
          Until the drains back up again?

Consolation (No. 9)

The eyes are shyly stricken:
                a momentary expression
Rests on their neighbouring world, with a sudden mood

Like storm-light, when it turns
Bricks to copper,   green
                     copper to blue.

Glossiness over the flint of these open lanes,
Caught up—gratuitous value, in a strong
Charge of things. For example, and not the best.

The mermaid rides, not staggering but singing,
These various favours.

The Moselle

passages from the Mosella *of Ausonius (4ᵗʰ century A.D.)*

Greenest of creatures,
   up your left and right
Ridges garnished aromatically
With vines;
   coated along the slopes
Of tender sides with turfy reaches;—

Ship-bearing as seas,
   but sliding river-like
With a declining run; in lucid volume
Rivalrous with broad, capacious lakes;

Peer to rills and becks
   in excitation; smart
Challenger to any chilly spring
For a pure cup;
    little runnel,
Gush of the fountain:
   what does either claim?—

Rivers, lakes, and the two-way refluent sea,
Ebbing and flooding: has any any merit
Wanting in you?

    *

You prosecute a most unruffled lapse:
Singular, placid course. No mumble of wind
Furrows your top; rocks offer no vexation;

Burbling shallows never jostle you by
In tearing urgency; no islands jut
Obtrusive   in the middle of your level:

A blemish on your name if any crag
Rose to divide and check your going,
Bother your bearing,   its
         mobile repose.

             *

I can see you, sometimes,
         checking yourself out:
How you admire
         your own recursive passage,
Seeming often as though you thought
Its proper flow, its glide,
         too slow, too idle, almost.

Grown in slime, ungainly sedge
Is not allowed to lace
         your banks; you never spill
To either side, in the fashion of lazier rivers,
Sludgy frontiers:

               cleanly go down the steps
That lead to your edge.

             *

Let those who lack
    Imagination

Pay for conspicuous
        Pavements of
Mosaic—lay out
        Expansive floors

Of lucent marble
        In panelled halls.

                For me (with a little
Sneer at what can be had for a stupid price),

I shall devote my admiration
To the present specimen of Nature's work,
Far from the nauseous bodings that annoy
People of prodigal taste;

But where an exuberant poverty
Wantonizes, happy in its free,
Ever-renewed expense.

Here, solid sands invest   the humid shores:
The press of approaching soles
Leaves   no lasting figure to record them.

                *

Through your smooth back
Your deep, pellucid spaces

(River keeping no secrets)
        can be seen.

Now the delicate air
Relaxes, clear and easy:

Well-contented breezes
Stir no barrier through the vacancy:

With vision reaching down to intimate parts,
We make out solid bodies sunk.
Your innermost retreats
Float visible,
            the waters going softly—
Flow with merest liquid
            showing in tinted light
Scattering images,
            diffusive forms:

The way the wrinkled sand
            is raked by the nimble currents;

The way the nodding grasses
Shudder tenderly,
Down in your greeny basement.

The driven weeds, beneath
            their own indigenous wave
Suffer continually its vibrancy.

                    *

Pebbles glance in the light
            and go to ground again.
The sand is shifting and sifting,
            the green moss peeping.

Wide Caledonian shores lie bared
To British eyes
When fleeing tides

Leave the dark seaweed naked in the day,
And the pink corals and candescent pearls
(Oysters' seeds), delights
          of finders and buyers—

Lapping under well-stored waves,
Illusive jewellery mocks our human vogues:

As plainly as that,
               down in the blithe Moselle
Herbs of no single tone
               veil and denude
The little stones mixed up among their roots.

                    *

Well, there's something to look at,
               free to eyes that look:

The glaucous river redisplays
The massed opacity of hills,

So it seems the slipping waters go
Bosky with adopted leaves;
As if the sprigs
          of shooting vines
Grew in the river.
                    ... The colour on its shine:—
When Venus comes, compelling shadows of night,
And splashes out the greenery
Of mirrored hills over Moselle.—

The hunching summits
Swim there whole,
In curling quivers;

Distant branches eddy there: the clusters
Fatten across the face of a polished wave.

The boatman feels the trick: eyes down,
As, one by one,
                    slip under them   the tendrils
Stiffened with sap: he floats

        Alone in the tree-bark vessel
        Far out in the water

Where the copied hill confounds itself with the river,
And the river fits itself
        with the limits of the shadows.

            *

When the bare sun floods down
With all a sun-god's heat,
He spills in the glassy course

The shapes of boys aboard their boats:
Wriggling forms of bodies upside-down.

As they repeat their stroke to left and right,
Throwing their weight to alternating oars,
The river renders   watery counterfeits
Of corresponding souls.
The boys take pleasure in their duplicates,
Lured by the fallacies the river returns.

So, before showing off
        her well-adjusted hair,
When grown-ups   for the first time
Prop up   for a little girl
The widely-shining,
        deep-inquiring mirror,
And gladly she discovers a novel game,
Seeing, she feels,
        a real, a sisterly face:

On gleaming metal, gives
        her unrequited kisses:
Fumbles there to affix
        her own deflected pins,
And catches at that brow,—
And means to run her hands in the dark curls;

Likewise, they, on their boats,
Drawn by these teasing idols,
Savour the figures, false and doubtfully true.

                *

The wet catch dances on the arid rocks,
Quakes at the lethal missiles
Of the sunlight-bearing day.

Under its native waters, it knew strength.
Sapped in our atmosphere,
Life weakens in the element it gasps.

The invalid body pulses now
With indolent palpitations, torpid tail
Suffering terminal tremors, and the lips

No longer meet:
          the fish expels
The air it takes   by yawning gills,
Rejecting in breath what brings it to this death.

Reminds me of bellows, when they blow
To nourish workers' fires,
And the woollen valve cavorts in the chamber of beech,
And its blinking aperture sucks in, by turns,
And hinders there   the wind it snatches.

But I have seen fish convulse
Under the closing pressure of death, collect
Their spirit, hurl themselves   into mid-air,
To give their tumbling bodies headlong back
To the river beneath,
Possessing again
The waters of which they almost had despaired.

                    *

The Sura—no
          low-born degenerate,
Itself enlarged
          by the bulk of two other streams—
Hurries to slip beneath your waves
And gratify you with its sum
          of intercepted waters:

Nobler involved in you, become Moselle,
Than if it poured back to parental Sea
A negligible mouth.

Tributaries race
To reach your side, to lick
Softly against you their
      submissive waters:

Rapid Celbis, known for its fish;
Erubris, rolling stones of mills
With flying revolutions in the corn,
And forcing strident saws
      through blocks of luminous marble,
Hearing continual noise from either bank.

I have nothing to say about the lank Lesura,
Nothing about the tenuous Drahonus.
What can I do with Salmona's beggarly dribble?

Saravus, floating ships
      on its wave-resounding mass,
Has been for some time in my sights—
With all the draperies of its robe   out loose,
Long drawing out its stream, so it might devolve
Its tired limits into you, beneath
The walls of Imperial Trier;

And, last, the Alisontia that slides
Lightly, through the fields of fattening regions,
Skimming the fruitful lips of its domain.

A thousand others—each in the urge
Of its own persistent and peculiar impulse—
Want to be yours: the end of their ambition,
The satisfaction of their inborn humour;
These impatient streams.

Fancypiece (III)

Leisurely waters stealing out of days
    Busy with other concerns—
Rivers that pick out pathways in the woods,
Naked over the huge untended fields,
Slipping over the farms
          their slack, irriguous streaks,

Exhibit, sometimes, at an idle glimpse
A length of definite, un-
          deliberate trails,
And may persuade the otherwise-tired mind
To search in them for accidental solutes,
Sifting, like a panner after gold,
Accumulations from the taken
          way: the channel floors'
Subjacent, half-known unexpectedness,
    Thickening, deepening;

The burdens flooded in from solid ground;
The clean attrition of rock edge; all
    Dark effluvia.

But wash it all back in, let it find an end,
A period, all arriving in the space
    Of water thick with coral,—
Where forthright into open ease infuse
Whatever freights are then free-carried of these
    Candid obliquities,

Drifting into promiscuous
Inconsequence, and lost, or else
Catching, collecting, feeding, building up
Show-tinted, less-than-candid honesties,
Worked upon, worked upon, in the tidal sweep,
In a living artifice, a growing
                              artifice of living.

Each in the spreading lune of a quiet bay,
    Not haunted much for gain,
Pours out;
              and the sediments of other earth—
Oversea-borne deposits—come to accost
The tributes from our still-uncharted home,
And feed, with them, the animate branches there,
The polyp antlers waving at the moon:

An architecture live and petrified,
A currency of roving and rooted things
Inhabiting the permeable peace
    This outlaw place affords.

Notes

The poems derived from Latin and Italian need no explanation, but something ought to be said about the two Hawaiian poems. My versions, which were labours of love during the first 'lockdown' of 2020 (when, surrounded by the fenlands of Cambridgeshire, I was longing for the landscapes of my childhood) are not intended as literal translations, but poetic paraphrases. They can carry no authority, since I neither speak nor read Hawaiian, though affectionately familiar with its sound and with certain words and phrases. I have made much use of the *Hawaiian Dictionary* and the primer of *Hawaiian Grammar* compiled in both cases jointly by Mary Kawena Pukui and Samuel H. Elbert, and can only hope that I have not gone too far astray. The grammar of Hawaiian, especially in the poetic idiom, is often highly ambiguous.

The piece offered here under the title 'Hawaiian Fragment' is from a passage recorded by the Hawaiian historian John Papa I'i (1800-1870), who does not name a source. See I'I, *Fragments of Hawaiian History*, trans. Mary Kawena Pukui, ed. Dorothy B. Barrère (Bishop Museum Press, Honolulu, 1959), p. 177. I have relied on the translator's version as the basis for my understanding (such as it is) of the original.

The song from which I translate 'Mist of Ka'ala' is collected in *Nā Mele o Hawai'i Nei*, ed. Samuel H. Elbert and Noelani Mahoe (University of Hawaii Press, Honolulu, 1970), where no author is named. It is 'postmissionary'. In making my own version I have relied upon these editors' plainer translation and have taken the liberty of varying slightly the refrain. Ka'ala is the highest mountain on the island of O'ahu (cf. 'The Wai'anae Range'). I used to be driven past it almost daily. In Hawaiian tradition, land-shells—snails of various kinds—were said to sing gently in the night. Coolness and rain in Hawaiian poetry often have associations rather different from those which English poetry, on the whole, might lead one to expect.

By the time this book goes to press, both Hawaiian poems will have appeared in *Modern Poetry in Translation*. I am grateful to the editors for allowing me to reprint them here.

The numbered 'Consolations' continue the series—not to be regarded as a sequence—begun in my previous collection. The reference to Stevie Nicks in 'Uncertain Light' is quite as conscious as those to Dryden's Virgil. And, whatever the sentiment of the 'Plague-Year Epistle', I *have* in fact met with some amiable people in the 'groves'. Some have even been amicable. Could that be another one there, among the dark shrubs? Fond hope.

Take it, if the question matters, that the old friends are several. 'There are so many deaths', Burne-Jones is supposed to have said to Frances Horner, 'besides the pale face which looks in at the door one day'.

The book is dedicated affectionately to the various people, including several of my students, who have aided my spiritual flotation through the social privations of this trying year.

A.W., 2020, 2021